SIMPLE PATTERNS COLORING BOOK

CRYSTAL
COLORING BOOKS

ISBN-13: 978-1546479352
ISBN-10: 154647935X

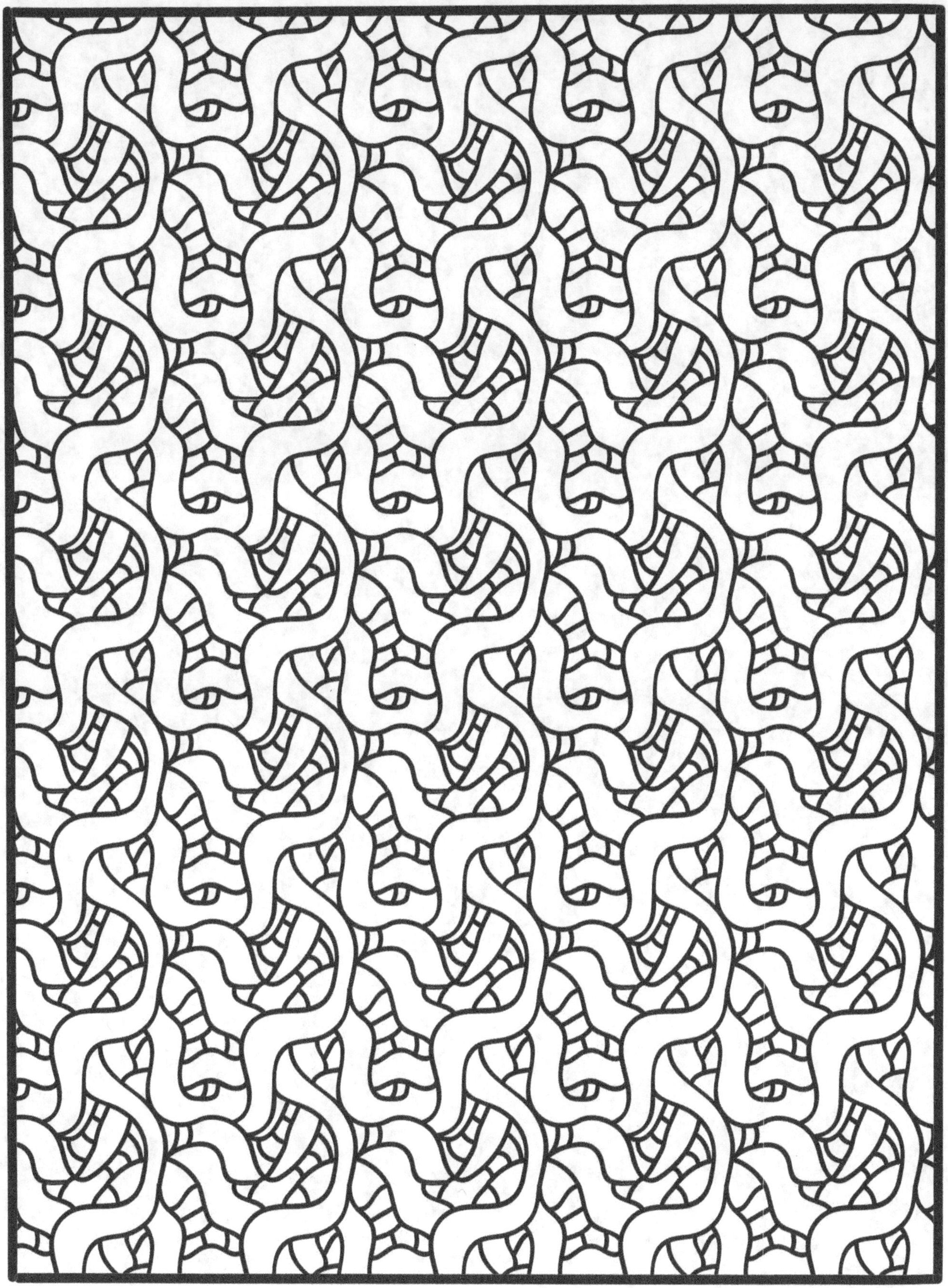

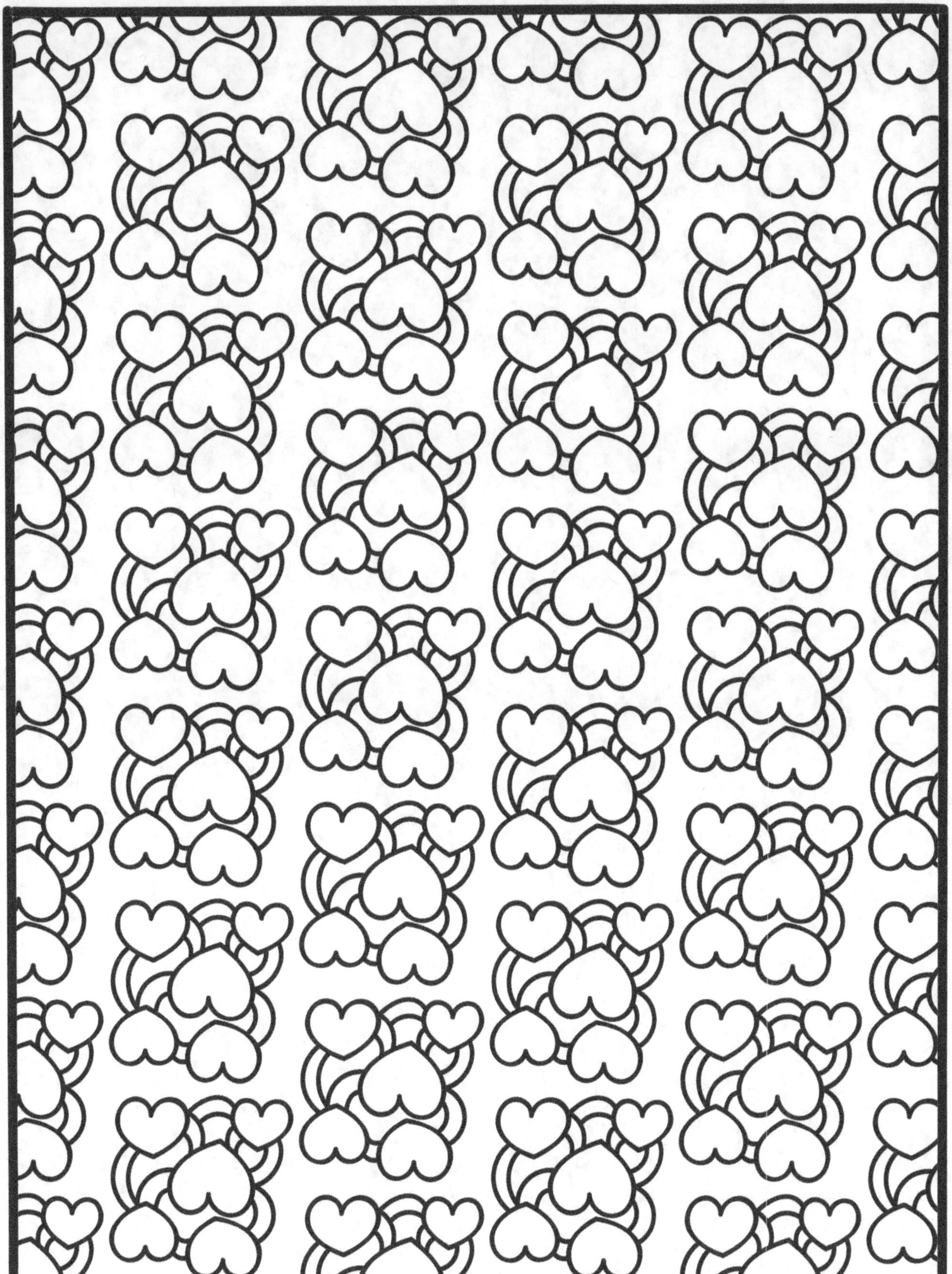

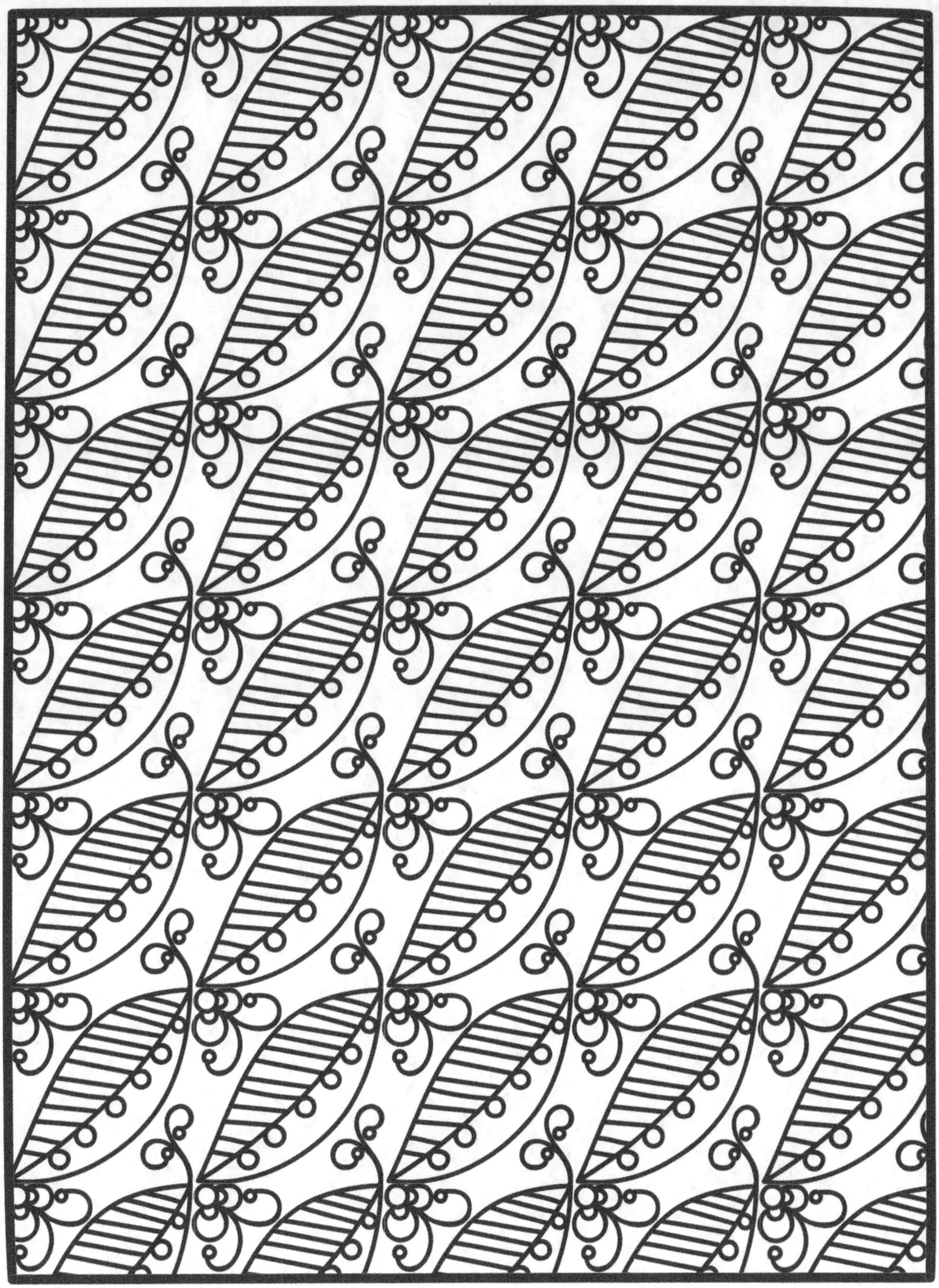

COLOR TEST PAGE

COLOR TEST PAGE

www.ingramcontent.com/pod-product-compliance
Lightning Source LLC
Chambersburg PA
CBHW081559280526
45788CB00011B/3515
9781546479352